Play Again

God's Love in Every Season

Table of Contents

It's funny how babies have to learn how to walk, but they never have to learn how to be held. The natural longing to be cradled is something beyond what we can teach. The desire to be held is eternally etched into our hearts. Even in our first moments of life, we're held intimately by the ones who carried us into this world. There's a sense of security and love when a child is swooped up in their parents' arms and carried. Before we can ever crawl, walk, or run through life, we must first reach up and allow ourselves to be carried.

Assuredly, I say to you, whoever does not receive the kingdom of God as a little child will by no means enter it." And He took them up in His arms, laid His hands on them, and blessed them.
Mark 10:15-16 NKJV

I've always been terrified of holding babies. My mind seems to jump to every possible bad thing that could happen while I'm holding them. What if I accidentally drop them? What if I hold them too tight? Worst of all. . . what if they don't like me? Okay, maybe that's not actually the worst thing that could happen, but it's pretty high on the list. Once I manage to trudge my way through my own imagination, actually holding and carrying a baby, a young and precious life, is an incredible experience. It's still terrifying in a sense, and I do usually still carry the worry of being thrown up on, but there's a sense of awe and wonder that comes over most of us when we connect with a new life. Whether it's their tiny hands and feet, their beautiful little eyes taking in the world around them, their sense of curiosity and whimsey, or their "new baby smell," we get overtaken by love and joy just being around them. We often feel our hearts swell with delight by a baby's gleaming purity and radiant trust.

We see ourselves in them. Maybe not as we are now, but we see what we long to be. There seems to be a reflection of our own innocence and love for life. When we look into the eyes of a newborn child, we look into the eyes of what we were created to be. We see a child who is loved beyond measure and cared for no matter what. This is our natural state. Throughout life, we manage to stray far away from this idea, but the seemingly small, realistically world-shattering moments of holding a child remind us of who we are. We have a Father looking at us exactly as we look at these little ones. The love that overtakes our hearts is a trait passed down from Him. God wants to remind you that this is the way He views you no matter what. Always. Even when it seems impossible for you to see it through your own eyes, you are God's beloved child.

Can you imagine God looking at you like a proud, loving parent looks down at their own child lying preciously in their hands? Can you imagine Him picking you up when you cry out or carrying you on His shoulder until you fall asleep? This is who He is. This is the heart that He has for His children. There are so many ways that we can look at God: an all-powerful being, the creator of the universe, the ruler of Heaven. Jesus' favorite way of looking at God, though, is a Father. He always refers to God as our Father, and he always makes sure we know that we are His children.

And He took them up in His arms

It can be hard to visualize God as a loving father who wants to carry you, but I'd like to paint a picture of what God the Father looks like in our lives. Imagine a father reaching down for you to take you out of your car seat. Your eyes are still fuzzy from falling asleep in the car, but you start to feel a warm summer breeze caress your face, and you hear the noises of laughing and playing coming from the park. It all seems so foreign, and you're not sure what to make of it, but your father is holding you close, and that's the only thing that matters. You look up and see the smile on his face as he starts walking you around the park. This is what life looks like when we humbly and lovingly let God father us and carry us. Life is simply a walk with God.

It takes a lot of trust to be carried by someone. Babies stretch their arms out toward their mother or father because they know in their heart that they are loved by their parents, and if mom or dad is carrying them, they'll be safe. Do we truly know in our hearts that we're safe in God's arms? When life is good and we've been on our best behavior, it surely seems like a wonderful place to be. What about when life gets messy, or maybe we feel like we haven't been the best version of ourselves? It may seem much scarier to be lifted into God's arms. Worse yet, it may seem like God doesn't even want to pick us up in those moments. It's hard to accept the safety of the Father's arms when the world has taught us so differently. Far too many times, we have to run away from someone's grasp out of fear, and we've become blinded to the idea of running into someone's grasp out of love. We all want to be held more than anything, but we're afraid to let most people, let alone God, close enough to reach us. Can I tell you something about your Father? He totally and utterly delights in carrying you when you're crying and fussing just as much as He does when you're sleeping or giggling. A father's love for his child does not rest on the performance of his child.

Why the park?

If God could take a walk with us anywhere, I think it would be through the park. There's something so beautiful and whimsical about the playing, learning, and growing in relationships that happens at the park. It mirrors our whole lives in an incredible way. There are times of laughter, times of pain and crying, and times of simply reflecting and taking it all in. When our Father is carrying us through the park, He looks out at all the activity going on around us, and He knows that those are places that we'll be one day. He already knows the plans ahead of us. We'll have seasons where we can play and enjoy ourselves with others, and we'll have seasons of frustration as He is trying to teach us how to share and get along better with others. He knows we'll grow into the parents who are trying to get their kids to calm down or clean the ice cream off of their shirt. He also knows that we will one day be the older man or woman who looks out and laughs at their grandchildren playing and wondering where all the time went. God knows what's ahead of us, but right now He is only concerned with the time He has to carry us close to Him.

If only we could feel how much God values the moments when he gets to carry us. He's excited to spend time with us, and there's nothing He loves more than when we let ourselves rest in His presence. He goes out of His way to pick us up, and if we allowed ourselves to lean in close enough and pause in His loving embrace, I'm sure we could even hear the beat of His heart that He has especially for us. We would be able to hear Him rejoice over us with singing. When we rest in His arms, we are soothed and quieted by His love. This is an incredibly intimate place that we must allow ourselves to reach. Your heart needs it. My heart needs it.

Don't be afraid to lean in close to your Heavenly Father and let Him carry you through the seasons that you can't quite walk on your own. It's not a burden for God to lift you up and care for you. He cares for all of us when we don't have the ability or capacity to care for ourselves. Rest in the fact that you have a loving Father who is willing to pick you up in His arms and remain close to you as you walk through life together. If you are mourning or struggling,

God delights in carrying you. If you need rest, God knows how to walk around with you and sing you to sleep. You may not know what the journey holds ahead, and there will be times when you don't recognize all the sights and sounds around you, but you can humbly trust that God has your best interest in mind and recognize His love for you as He carries you and lets His smile beam down on you.

I have a niece who could have won the award for "Most Heavy-Footed Toddler of All Time." If you have ever had a toddler in your family, you've probably felt the same way. Who knew such tiny feet could create such an echoing pitter-patter against the ground? Even though these tiny humans may not be very sneaky, they are extremely eager to see where their feet can take them. Younglings do not carry the most grace when they start taking steps of their own, but that's where a gentle hand to help pick them up and guide them can change everything. The grace that is beyond their ability is freely given to them through the help of a loving parent. In the areas in which they can't make it on their own or stumble and fall, they have loving hands to help them up. This is such a mirror image of how we all still walk today. All of us go through seasons of our lives and in our walks with God when we may not be running our best race or walking the most gracefully, but we're taking baby steps, and those are so much more important than we think.

I taught Ephraim to walk, Taking them by their arms; But they did not know that I healed them. I drew them with gentle cords, With bands of love, And I was to them as those who take the yoke from their neck. I stooped and fed them.
Hosea 11:3-4 NKJV

It's truly beautiful how much time we take to slow down and celebrate a baby's first steps. There's something incredibly adventurous about seeing a young life draw up the courage and excitement to take those first steps, and there's something wonderfully heartfelt about watching a proud parent take joy in their child's accomplishment. It's a moment that is never forgotten, and it's just the beginning of an incredible journey. God looks at you and takes joy in your baby steps in the exact same way a parent does for their child. He is absolutely delighted to slow down and celebrate the small, overlooked moments of your life. Our small steps are tremendously important to God. He cares about the details, and He loves being there with you through your baby steps in life.

It's kind of funny how we remember the baby steps so much more than most of the following ones. My parents couldn't describe what my steps were like six months ago, but they could joyfully describe what my first ones were like. The tiniest steps can create the greatest impact. God is proud of your tiny steps. He is extremely fond of the clumsy steps that most likely need His assistance. God celebrates those moments when you build up the strength and courage to initiate those first few baby steps, and He is more than happy to jump in and help you walk even farther. Your small steps matter to Him so much. He sees you growing, and He's fully aware of the effort that you put into those steps. They may not be the biggest steps, but they may be God's favorite ones.

Let's go back to the park for a bit. We've been carried by our Father so far on this walk, but now we experience this growing sense inside of us that we're ready to touch the ground below. We're not very strong or graceful, so we may stumble and fall if we try to take our first steps on our own. Our Father knows this. As a caring father does, He lets us down gently but remains holding on to both of our hands up above our head, guiding us forward with every step. He might even set our feet down on top of His shoes just to make sure we get used to the motions. Each small movement forward is completely under His control and guidance. There isn't a single step that He is not aware of, and He never doubts His ability to lead us. He is with us every step of the way. This is the God that we walk with. He is a good Father who cares about every step of our journey through this life.

He will not allow your foot to slip; He who keeps you will not slumber.
Psalm 121:3 NIV

Sometimes it feels like God has turned away from the everyday activities in our lives or that He's left so many of our problems up to us. You may have gone through a season with thoughts like, "God, why are you not helping me find a job?" Maybe you've even thought, "God, you haven't even been helping me lately. I keep asking for help, and you're still not here. I think I need to do this on my own." We've all ventured through those moments and those thoughts. We've all felt like maybe our problems, relationships, or even dreams just aren't important enough to bother God with. Maybe we're asking Him all wrong, or maybe He's just not listening. We feel alone. One of the most beautiful things about our heavenly Father is that He is always present even when it doesn't feel like it. He is always with you, and He is never bothered or ignorant to your times of need. When a toddler is stumbling and getting tripped up on their own legs, I'm sure they don't

recognize the help that they are truly
getting from a father who is guiding them
along the way. Through every tiny step,
through every loss of balance, and through
every worry of hitting the ground, God is
holding your hands, and He will not allow
your foot to slip.

Beauty in the Everyday

Baby steps do not only equate to
stumbling and being clumsy, but they also
represent the absolute beauty that is our
lives. When we think about the things that
have shaped us and left lasting impressions
on us, we typically think of big events in our
lives. We love reflecting on the huge turning
points in our lives that we feel have made
us who we are. We even love using them as
excuses for our behavior sometimes.
Though the large moments do have a
lasting impression on us, the things that
really shape who we are look a lot more like
every Monday morning. We might think our
lives look like a culmination of our biggest
achievements and milestones, but our lives
truly look more like how we love our
families, appreciate the moments we have
with those around us, and choose to spend
every single new day that we have.
As we grow older, it's incredible how
much more we see the value in the small
moments of our lives. I want to feel the
weight of importance in every face to face

conversation I have. I desire to be able to open my eyes to the small moments that will soon be memories. Above all else, I want to cherish the people who are around me most before it's too late. There's something in my heart telling me that if you're reading this, you probably desire the same thing too. We all wish we could recognize the good times before they are washed away. We all know someone we wished we would have hugged just a little bit longer. We all carry moments when we wish we would have said, "I love you." I never look back and think about gifts I wish I had gotten or awards I wish I had won. Like you, I look back and think about people. I think about those I love and the moments that we shared. These are what matter most.

There are so many everyday moments over our lifetimes that make us who we are. Who we played with on the playground when we were kids, the stories that our parents told us, our first jobs, and even how we spend a Saturday afternoon all create the story of who we are and the lives that we live. Even in the instances that don't feel special, God is walking with us and doing a new work in us. Isn't that incredibly assuring to know? God is with you during every family dinner equally as much as He is during church on Sunday. He walks with you during every moment that you may stress over bills, have car trouble, be in the middle of a fight with someone, or any other situation that His presence may feel lacking. He's there. God remains with you and for you through everything. He truly cares about every baby step because He truly cares about you.

We're constantly being given reminders that God is with us every step of the way. Your Father loves being involved in the details of your life, and every new day is His way of reaching out to show you. He's in every breathtaking sunrise, and the first light of each day can serve as a reminder of how close He is to us. He is with you in every laugh you share with friends, every hug you give a family member, every "I love you" that you choose to speak, every changed diaper, every song you sing along to with your car windows down, and every late night that you gaze at the stars shining down on you. Yeah, God is in the baby steps.

For I, the Lord your God, will hold your right hand,
Saying to you, 'Fear not, I will help you.'
Isaiah 41:13 NKJV

Most of us have probably heard our mom or dad say the phrase, "Hold my hand," when we were growing up. The tone of voice that they used, though, may have depended on our personal situations. If you ever heard this phrase followed by your full name, you may as well run the other direction. Regardless of whether it sounded frustrated or caring, that was the moment that all of us reached up and trusted our parents enough to grab a hold of their hand. There was something deep inside all of us, the same thing that still resonates deep within children today, letting us know that if mom or dad says, "Hold my hand," we should most likely follow their command. What is it inside all of us that told us, without a second thought, that we needed to follow that order and grab a hold of our caretaker's hand? Maybe it's fear: fear of being disciplined, fear of being taken away or lost, fear of our surroundings. It could be that, but I think it's probably something much deeper and foundational to our inner beings than fear.

There is no fear in love. But perfect love drives out fear, because fear has to do with punishment. The one who fears is not made perfect in love.
1 John 4:18 NIV

Love has the ability to take a hold of our hearts deeper than fear could ever dream. Why did we always seem to listen to our parents and take their hands in ours when they told us to? Because we loved them, and they loved us. This is the kind of love that allows roots to grow deep in our souls, allowing us to connect and grow with each other. Even though we are complicated, love is simple. Love is a person, love reaches out, and love holds your hand when you need it. Life ("the park") is full of so many distractions and so much noise; don't forget that throughout your entire walk, you have a Father next to you who knows exactly when you tell you, "Hold my hand." Luckily for us, His tone is never sharp or angry. He is never frustrated with us, and He won't pull us away to scold us. He just wants us to be by His side and to be safe. God wants us to experience walking through this life with Him the way it should be experienced. He is the fullness of love, and there's something inside all of us that inherently yearns to reach up for His hand. For some of us, we reach out to any hand that seems close to us. We don't fully grasp what it is that we're trying to hold on to, so we take hold of anything. It can be easy to grab onto things that lead us in the wrong direction, but there is One who loves us constantly and is desperately making a way for His hand to take hold of ours. His hand leads us to life and light.

The thief comes only to steal and kill and destroy; I have come that they may have life, and have it to the full.
John 10:10 NIV

These are the words of Jesus himself. God wants us to have life and have it to the full. Other translations show us that God wants us to have life *abundantly*. What does living life to the fullest look like to you? Is it getting that job you've always wanted? Could it look like marrying the person you always dreamed, or traveling the world to all the places you've always wanted to vacation? In reality, having life to the full simply looks like walking with our Father, no matter what season or situation we may find ourselves in. There is abundant joy in the presence of our loving Father. Again, even though we are complicated, love is simple. Experiencing the fullness of life will never depend on something or someone temporary. Full life comes from the One who created life. You may not have it all together or be anywhere close to where you want to be in life, but your Father is right there walking with you, providing you peace, joy, and strength always. Are you struggling with getting the job that you want? God is walking next to you saying, "Hold my hand." Are you living through a season of depression due to not being able to start that family you wanted so badly? God is walking next to you saying, "Hold my hand." Do you struggle with liking the person who looks back at you in the mirror? Your Heavenly Father is walking right next to you saying, "Hold my hand." God will never get tired of reminding you that you can reach out to Him at any time for anything. He won't force your hand toward His, but once you reach up, He delightfully joins hands with you and shows you a new way.

But he said to me, "My grace is sufficient for you, for my power is made perfect in weakness." Therefore I will boast all the more gladly about my weaknesses, so that Christ's power may rest on me.

When a parent reaches down to take their child's hand, it's because that parent knows the child is too weak to walk on their own. A parent provides strength, safety, and support. When we were all kids and wanted to go off and explore some new place on our own, the feeling of our mom or dad pulling on our hands in the opposite direction is actually what it looks like for someone's power to be made perfect in our weaknesses. Even in the midst of our bad decisions or distractions, there is a hand that pulls us back where we need to be. Back where we were meant to be. Our parents wanted us to be safe and follow close to them because they loved us and could be the strong ones when we were still weak. If you're a parent, you know the motive behind keeping your children close or restricting them from certain things is because you want the best for them. It's always out of love. This is the exact same type of love that God has for us, and when He reaches out for our hands when we are weak, that's actually when His power is made perfect. He's done this perfectly since the dawn of man. Since the time of Adam and Eve, we've been weak children who have needed to reach out to their Father for strength. We were made to need our Father. It doesn't bother Him to guide us or help us through any season of life. His grace is sufficient, and when He holds our hand and guides us, His power is made truly perfect.

It's hard to trust people, and this can make it difficult to reach out to God. We get scared to break down the walls that we worked so hard to build up, and we don't want to look weak when we're let down. Expectations hurt, but God isn't in the business of hurting us. He helps us when we can't help ourselves, and remarkably enough, He loves doing so. Trusting God shows absolute strength on our part, even when it means submission to Him out of weakness.

Sticky Hands

Let's change the pace here for a minute and get real. Kids' hands are kind of gross sometimes. Actually, a lot of the time. Children love to play in the dirt and grass, stick their fingers in their mouths, or go digging for gold. And what do most kids hate? Washing their hands. Though it may seem gross sometimes, children' love for dirtiness helps provide a great picture of what life looks like as we grow up. When we were kids, we weren't afraid of playing in the dirt. We weren't thinking about the cleanup that always came after; we were just enjoying the time we had to simply be. Without even recognizing it, we were "having life to the full." Now we've grown up, and the idea of being dirty is the worst thing a lot of us could imagine. We want to have it together. We want to be presentable. We don't want to have to be "cleaned." Can I ask you something, though? When you reach down to hold your child's hand and guide them, do you ever really care whether or not their hands are clean? When you're walking with one of your children, and you notice them falling away from your side, I doubt you examine the cleanliness of their hands before deciding to bring them back safely by your side. You just want your child next to you, knowing that they have you there to keep them safe. This is how our Heavenly Father's heart works when He walks with us through life. We often get so ashamed of how low or downright dirty we feel, and we'd rather do anything in the world to try to pick ourselves up before letting God help us. We don't want to be judged for not being clean. We don't want to be abandoned for not being strong enough or good enough. God doesn't care how dirty your hands are. He's not checking you to make sure that you're clean and proper enough before He decides to grab your hand and pull you in close to Him. God wants you close to Him simply because you are His child and He loves you.

Have life to the fullest. Walk through the park with your Father, and know that even through all the sights, sounds, detours, and stops along the way, you two will always be on this journey together.

We're all taking this walk with Him, and there's absolutely nothing wrong with the fact that all of us need to reach up and hold His hand.

There's something so incredibly indistinguishable and nostalgic about the sound of an ice cream truck playing the same jingle that we all grew up loving. When I was growing up, there was nothing in the world quite as satisfying as the taste of a frosty ice cream cone after a long afternoon of play. It was obviously so much better than any ice cream at home, but it wasn't just the flavors or various ways that the sweet treats were served that really caught mine and all of our love and attention. It's something about the anticipation and the experience of hearing that music and running just to catch the beloved ice cream man's attention. Whatever and whoever I was playing with were quickly left behind as I ran toward the sound of that jingle.

As a young connoisseur of ice cream, price was never a concern for me. . . as long as mom or dad was close by. Luckily for me, they always seemed to keep up pretty well when I spotted the ice cream truck. Sometimes, it was even their idea to go to the ice cream truck in the first place. Now that I've grown up more, I've started to realize that even adults occasionally need a childlike journey for ice cream in the midst of their hectic and worrisome days, but that may be a different lesson for a different time. The point here is that I always had a provider with me. I had a loving parent by my side who truly enjoyed seeing the delight on my face when I got to have that experience.

And my God shall supply all your need according to His riches in glory by Christ Jesus.
Philippians 4:19 NKJV

It's easy to see how a parent provides for a child in something as simple as buying them an ice cream cone, but the provision of God is something much deeper and more sustaining than just supplying us with material things. Just as a father cares more about the delight of their child rather than caring about the ice cream itself, our Heavenly Father cares about the delight of His children rather than caring about the temporary things that come and go throughout our lifetimes. When God supplies all of our needs, it doesn't necessarily mean he gives us new stuff. Our true, eternal needs are met when we are in close relationship with the Father. Walking with Him, talking to Him, and trusting in Him are ways that our hearts and souls can be filled with what we really need. All of us are created uniquely and beautifully different, but the very core of our needs is typically the same. We all need love, a sense of purpose, peace, and inner strength. No matter what background or belief, these are the inner needs that we have that seem to connect every person and transcend all borders, religion, age, or anything else. Our need for these is all met through close relationship with our Father.

We can often find ourselves going through daily activities or even entire seasons of life without engaging with God, and it always seems to result in frustration, depleted strength, or even feeling completely lost. This inner turmoil is due to the fact that we've separated ourselves from our one true source. We forget our value when we stop talking to our Father who always tells us worthy and loved we are. We start getting angrier and more frustrated with people and situations around us when we stop trusting God to be there with us to provide peace. Being close to the Father gives us a direct supply of what our souls need. When we lean into God, He can start to transform areas of our hearts that we thought were unreachable.

There are things that I'm embarrassed to ask God for, and there are even sometimes that I haven't trusted God enough to ask Him for help. I believe most of us at some point have had the fear that if we unload all of our baggage or problems on God, He will either look at us differently or love us less. We've had this happen with the people around us, so we have taught ourselves to expect it to happen with God too. "I can't ask God to do that. It's too much of a bother." Almost all of us have been there. "I can't ask God for help because I haven't been good enough to deserve His help." These are the thoughts that start to push us further and further away from the one person who cares for us the most. It's hard for us to fathom that someone could not only care for us so intimately after knowing all of our downfalls, but also that someone could see all of our areas of weakness and need and somehow supply our souls with the love, rest, and encouragement that they need.

The incredible news is that no matter how low you may be or embarrassed you may feel to ask God for help, He already knows what you need before you ask. He knows, and He is ready to listen to you and supply your needs. When a child wants something or needs help, you can see it on their face far before they ever have to say a single word. When a young one is struggling with reaching something or finishing a task, you can see very plainly in their behavior that they need someone stronger than them to come along and lift their burden. When a child's face lights up at the sound of the ice cream truck coming down the road, it's a fairly easy guess that they'll be craving whatever sweet treats they can get their hands on. Before you say anything, God already knows. He simply wants you to trust Him enough to lean in and ask Him for what you need. There shouldn't be any fear in going to your Father who loves you perfectly and asking Him for help or provision. He knows you need it, and He delights in supplying your needs.

When I was in preschool, an ice cream truck always came once a week while we were playing outside. I remember playing tag or Simon Says out on the playground and suddenly hearing the ice cream truck roll around the side of the building and meet us right there where we were playing. Even though it came every single week, it always seemed like a pleasant surprise. It was by far the most exciting thing that happened each week. God bless the teachers that agreed to give sugary ice cream to children that were probably already too full of energy anyway.

There are so many wonderful things that I remember about this preschool. I remember the music that got played for us, the firetruck that we got to explore, and all the whispering way too loudly during nap time. One of the best memories though, and the one thing that came every week, was ice cream day.

I will never know the name of the man who came to my preschool every week to give us ice cream, but I will always remember the impact he had on my childhood. These simple moments of provision and receiving good gifts seem to stay with us. We cherish the gifts and the people who give them to us, and even more so, God cherishes the fact that we can enjoy these small reminders of him. Ice cream guy, if you're reading this: thank you.

So do not worry, saying, 'What shall we eat?' or 'What shall we drink?' or 'What shall we wear?' For the pagans run after all these things, and your heavenly Father knows that you need them. But seek first his kingdom and his righteousness, and all these things will be given to you as well. Therefore do not worry about tomorrow, for tomorrow will worry about itself. Each day has enough trouble of its own.
Matthew 6:31-34 NIV

Can I give you some simple advice? Never value the ice cream cone more than the father who provided it for you. The reason I have so many heartwarming memories of spending summer days playing and enjoying ice cream with my dad is because I had him there to watch over me and provide for me. If you want to know what this passage of scripture in Matthew 6 looks like, it's being so wrapped up in enjoying time with your Father and delighting in those afternoons with Him that you're not even thinking about what tomorrow may bring. You may not know how that meeting will go, or it might seem like the bills coming up are going to be too much to handle, but for today, seek spending time with your Father who loves you, and trust that He is going to take care of you. Worrying about tomorrow only steals the joy from today. Have that play time with God. Laugh with Him, grow closer to Him, and maybe even get some ice cream on your shirt while you're at it.

I'll admit it: I've been embarrassed to be seen with my parents before. Mom and dad, if you're reading this, I'm sorry. During my early teenage years, I considered going to the store with my parents to be the worst form of torture. I remember speeding ahead when we got into the store, so it would seem like I wasn't there with them. I know, it's pretty convincing for a thirteen-year-old to try to pull off independently making their way to the store. Looking back, I've noticed one constant theme throughout those years. The way that I viewed my parents never actually changed who they were; it only changed who they were to me. Even though I wanted to run ahead and separate myself from my parents, it didn't change the fact that they are indeed my parents, and it certainly did not change the way that they saw me.

Sometimes when we run away from a certain person or situation, it's not really because of them. It's because of us. Pain has a way of taking us away from the very things we need. Pain can often lead to distance, distance to fear, and fear to isolation. Have you ever backed away from somebody, not necessarily because of anything they did, but because you were hurting and scared of connection? We often feel like the pain that we are experiencing is unique to us, and nine times out of ten, this will lead to us running away from those who could help us most. We don't want to feel embarrassed. We don't want to feel the weight of our shame hit the shoulders of someone else. We don't want to be crushed under judgment or condemnation. So, what do we do instead? We run. It seems much less scary to run away from our problems rather than walk hand in hand with someone else directly through our problems.

The power of connection always triumphs the power of pain. There are so many times in life when it feels like we're alone, or it feels like we need to be alone. The beautiful news is that we're never truly alone. Throughout all the highs and lows in life, we are constantly surrounded by people that God has specifically placed in our lives to share our experiences with. God always walks directly with us, but He also loves inviting friends over for us to play with. The people in your life matter, and your Father specifically placed them around you in order to care for you and comfort you in those moments when everything inside of you is telling you to run.

What's the draw?

Why do we seem so naturally inclined to run ahead and try to escape what's weighing us down in life? Well, running ahead can seem like it's putting us in control. When I put distance between myself and my parents at the store, it felt like I was in control of how other people saw me and how my shopping experience would go. We want to create the image that we have it all together, and we want to feel in control of our experience of life. We don't have that burden on our shoulders, though. We aren't called to be in control of our lives; we're simply called to trust God in every step. The pressure of being in control isn't on us. We can look up to our Father and know that He is working all things out for our good, and He knows what is best for us.

Running ahead also creates a distraction from the trials that we may be facing. If we can sprint somewhere new, we don't have to fret over the old. We have this idea that maybe we can leave our problems or our identities behind. You're not created to leave your identity behind, and all of us have pain that we simply can't run away from and expect to have a healthy soul. The simplicity of running away creates a fantastic temporary relief, but time after time, it proves to leave a long-lasting hole in our hearts where genuine healing needs to take place. There's no substitute for authentic care. The absence of being cared for eats us up inside, and it changes the way we look at others and ourselves. Don't believe the lie that running will create something better. The truth is that there is a God who cares for you so much that He would rather walk with you through every dirty, broken situation than to see you run away from your healing.

A harsh truth.

In the scripture that was included at the beginning of the chapter, Luke 15, Jesus describes the story of a young son who wants his inheritance from his father immediately, so he can leave his father behind and go live the way he wishes. The son would have rather gone to a far-off land where he knew absolutely nobody than spend one more day in his father's house. The boy in the story seems so selfish and careless because of his actions, but can I admit something harshly true about myself? Sometimes I don't want to be with my Father either. I said it. There are days, weeks, or even seasons in my life that I don't want to be with God. I find myself relating to this young son so much, because I have been in his shoes. Sometimes I would rather run than face God. I would rather go to a far-off land than sit and work out my struggles with my Father. There are times when it feels easier to run. Remember what I said about my own parents, though. The way I viewed them didn't actually change the character of who they are. The same can be said about our relationship with God.

When I feel like running away from God, it's always because I have forgotten to see Him for who He truly is. Maybe circumstances around me have skewed my view on Him for a bit, or even my own emotions toward myself project on my view towards God. In every situation that I think He's not good or He's not there, He is. Every instance that I've wanted to turn from him and walk down my own path is because of the fact that I lost sight of the love that my Heavenly Father truly has for me. Maybe some of these words are resonating with you right now. We all seem to form our own views on who God must be depending on the season of life around us. When life is full of peace and provision, it's easy to see God as a good Father who cares. When life seems cold and like it's falling apart, though, we tend to wonder where God has gone. This is when we can easily start to feel like we must take matters into our own hands and run ahead.

Where can I go from your Spirit? Where can I flee from your presence? If I go up to the heavens, you are there; if I make my bed in the depths, you are there. If I rise on the wings of the dawn, if I settle on the far side of the sea, even there your hand will guide me, your right hand will hold me fast. If I say, "Surely the darkness will hide me and the light become night around me," even the darkness will not be dark to you; the night will shine like the day, for darkness is as light to you.

For you created my inmost being; you knit me together in my mother's womb. I praise you because I am fearfully and wonderfully made; your works are wonderful, I know that full well.
Psalm 139:7-14 NIV

No matter how far or fast we may run, God is a much better runner than us. In every low season where we're constantly pushing others away, God is constantly pressing in. He doesn't turn His back on you when you turn your back on Him. God is not the root of your pain, and I promise He truly cares enough for you to reach out and heal those wounds. You don't have to run from His shame because there is none. You don't have to flee from His condemnation, because He condemns absolutely nobody who is in Christ Jesus. God is a good Father, and no matter how far or how many times you may run, He is always overjoyed at the thought of having you in His loving arms again.

Growing up, all of our parents typically knew more about what we were getting into than we thought they knew. In the times when it felt like we evaded their attempts to get close to us, they usually had an awareness of what was really going on. No matter what our words may say, we typically have what we're really going through painted all over our faces. A parent can see when their child is going through something. God sees everything that we're going through, and no matter how much we think we are doing things on our own, we're not really alone. When we run ahead due to pride, God is always right behind us. When we run ahead due to fear, God is always ahead of us. His love never leaves us, and it never forsakes us. Even when we don't want to be with Him, He still longs to be close to us. Our Father is the one who reaches out, climbs mountains, searches valleys, and crosses oceans just to connect with us. We all run a little bit ahead of our parents sometimes, but the important thing is recognizing that they never let themselves get as far as it seems. You might be in a season where you're running, but as you're reading this, God is keeping pace right there with you.

When I arrived in the wonderful world of middle school, I quickly realized how much I hated the bell. You know the bell. The one that signifies that you're late to the whole class as you come bolting through the door mere seconds after its finish. The five-minute period between my classes soon became a race against time. I even learned to overcome obstacles along the way like teachers who keep you after the bell or wet floors in busy hallways. I think the biggest lie I was ever told throughout my teenage years was, "You have time between class to use the bathroom." If you're a teacher who is reading this, we'll agree to disagree. Middle school was more like bladder training camp. It's actually pretty incredible that I never once peed my pants in school, but I definitely missed a lot of lessons due to my focus being... elsewhere.

You could say I adapted pretty well. I perfected my speed walking, and I learned how to get on a teacher's good side just in case I decided to show up to class fashionably late. Middle school most definitely moved at a different rate than what I was used to. I'm not exactly sure when my life started to feel so busy and rushed, but it definitely feels like this scramble to get to class eight times a day may have been the start of it.

When did we all start to get so rushed with our daily lives? It sort of feels like it just happened one day. It can seem as though our lives leaped from merely playing with others and enjoying each moment of every day to packing our schedules so much that we don't even allow ourselves time to breathe. We're in a hurry. This creates a problem for us when we end up surrounded by people, places, and things that are not in a hurry like we are. We wonder what's wrong with the person who is happily taking their time; meanwhile, we're collapsing under the weight of our own business. When we're busy, it's easy for us to want other people to catch up to where we're at. A deeper desire of our hearts, though, is that we want God to catch up to us when we're busy. So many of us are living fast and feel like we're serving a God who is simply too slow.

The Lord is not slow to fulfill his promise as some count slowness, but is patient toward you, not wishing that any should perish, but that all should reach repentance.
2 Peter 3:9 ESV

God works at a different pace than we do. He is a God who is always working on our behalf and constantly making a way for us, but He is absolutely never in a rush to do so. There are many times in our lives when we feel as though God just isn't working on our side, or maybe He's too slow to fix the problems that we have right now. We've become so accustomed to getting our food faster, checking the weather faster, driving faster, and working faster that it can sometimes feel like we have outpaced God. It feels as though maybe He's not able to keep up. You might even live through seasons when it feels like God has forgotten about you. Even when it feels like God has fallen behind, He is truly ahead of us more than we could ever imagine. He knows what today will bring. Actually, He knows what each day will bring. Instead of insisting that God hurry up to work with our plans, let's not be afraid to slow down and meet Him where He's at. I promise that wherever God is, we want to be. Life is so much better with someone by your side. Why not let the Creator of all be the one you allow close to you?

God hasn't forgotten about you. He hasn't forgotten about all the prayers that you've prayed to Him, and He never forgets any of the promises that He makes. He is good and faithful to remember you and take care of you. You don't have any deadlines or expectations to meet before God wants to be with you. He delights in being with you no matter where you're at, what you've done, or how you feel. God's not your boss; He's your Father. There is no rush in the time that we spend with Him. There will always be certain things in our lives that we desperately need God to move quickly on, but this shouldn't be what the majority of our walk with God looks like. We need certain things from Him from time to time, but what we need most of all is connection to Him. This is where peace comes into our hearts no matter what situation we're in. When we're connected to Him, it's where strength and courage take over our souls. Even when life is hectic and you can't seem to catch a break, don't be afraid to take the time to connect with God.

He doesn't need to be impressed.

There's a wonderful innocence in seeing someone's eyes light up as they show you something that they're so very proud of. When I was growing up, I would always get excited and try to rush my friends and family when I wanted to show them something I was thrilled about. All of us have a deep inner desire to be noticed when we've done things that we're proud of. We want someone else to also be proud of us. We long for others to share in the joy that we feel at that moment. That longing to be seen by others is truly a beautiful part of our human connection. We get so exhilarated to show others a part of ourselves, and the excitement of it drives us to call out, "C'mon, let's go! I have something to show you!" Kids often want to show off their new toys or whimsical new ways they've found to play. Teenagers love to show off the new clothes that they bought for the new school year. Adults even feel a rush of excitement to show off their promotions or accomplishments. It's wonderful when we feel an excitement and a rush to show others what we can do, but it can often lead to emptiness when others don't receive our joyous news the way that we want them to. It hurts not to be seen.

I think our longing to impress people leaks into our relationship with God. We get so used to basing our value on impressing other people, we feel like the only way that God will want to stay in relationship with us is if we impress Him, too. Maybe you aim to do good deeds so God will be proud of you. Sunday morning church could possibly be on your checklist to stay on God's good side. Maybe you're like me and feel like your relationship with the Father could be torn down if you fail too much. There's this secret fear inside of us that maybe God just couldn't possibly be proud of us. There's no way we could ever do enough or impress Him enough to earn His love.

That's exactly the point.

We love because he first loved us.
1 John 4:19 NIV

We're not created to impress God. Our relationship with our Heavenly Father is not determined by all of the good parts of ourselves that we can show to Him. We can never do enough to earn His love, and we're not expected to. He loved us first, and He will always love us. It's okay to drop the guards of our hearts with God. He created you with so much love in His eyes, and when He looks at you, He sees His son and daughter. When you look at your child, you don't determine all the right and wrong things they've done before considering whether or not they are your child. You know they are your child because you, out of love and longing to have them in your life, created them in your image. We are all created in God's image, carrying the love He has for us in our hearts. Your Father is in Heaven right now looking down at you with a beaming gaze of love. He is fixated simply on knowing you. You don't have to impress God to be seen by God.

This inner desire that we all have to be loved and accepted can only be filled by one thing: the love of a Father. The approval of others may feel good in the moment, but the disapproval of them seems to sting a lot longer. Luckily, your value is not in what you can accomplish. Your value comes from your Father, and there is nothing in the entire world worth more to Him than you. Again, God has not forgotten about you. You don't have to rush Him, and you certainly don't have to impress Him. It may seem simple, but that's the nature of how our Father works. Through the complex, the poetic, and the disorganized order of life, the message is always simple.

God loves you.

I've never broken any bones (so far), but I might actually be the king of cuts and bruises. "Graceful" and "agile" have never really been the right words to describe me. The fact that I've never broken a bone could truly be proof that God still works miracles. Truthfully, we're all a bit clumsy in our own ways. People are naturally gifted in finding new ways to get themselves hurt. Sometimes, life looks like band aids, casts, or even wheelchairs. We all get hurt every once in a while, but what do we do when it seems like we've been knocked down?

A few years back, I got in a car wreck that I thought was going to be the end of me. Spoiler alert: it wasn't. I had taken my old little silver Mazda on a road trip several hours away from home, and my evening was filled with mountain roads, beautiful views, and a sunset over the foothills of Arkansas that I will always remember. My journey back home was slightly less beautiful and nostalgic. About halfway home, the back tire on the right-hand side of the car completely blew out, sending me spinning off the interstate at about seventy-five miles an hour. Spinning in circles, my car bounced off the median a whopping six times, and I ended up landing somewhere in a grassy area between the two sides of the highway. After realizing I wasn't dead, I kind of felt like a Nascar driver who just spun into the wall and made the race interesting to watch. I felt pretty cool, but more than that, I felt a lot of pain. Luckily, a state trooper came out to help me, and even more luckily, I was able to walk away from that accident without going to the hospital.

By the grace of God, I didn't have to be put in a hospital or fight for my life after that accident, but the road to recovery had some unexpected bumps along the way. I was bruised up and scraped from all the hits and broken glass. My head was quite a bit more fuzzy than usual for a while. What I didn't realize at first, though, is that the impact of that wreck left me with a good case of whiplash. I went months and months of feeling pain and stiffness in my neck that made it hard to even hold my head up sometimes. Most nights, sleeping through the ache was a challenge, and I found myself with more headaches and stiffness throughout the day. I was in pain for a season, but this could not stop me from choosing to get better. It was a bump in the road, but it wasn't the end of the race.

Therefore, since we are surrounded by such a great cloud of witnesses, let us throw off everything that hinders and the sin that so easily entangles. And let us run with perseverance the race marked out for us, fixing our eyes on Jesus, the pioneer and perfecter of faith. For the joy set before him he endured the cross, scorning its shame, and sat down at the right hand of the throne of God. Consider him who endured such opposition from sinners, so that you will not grow weary and lose heart.
Hebrews 12:1-3 NIV

Unexpected pain is a part of life, but this pain always tends to bring out unexpected strength. People have a beautiful ability to overcome incredible obstacles. We hear about people that have gone through great seasons of pain or were left disabled for their entire lives, and it makes the hairs on our arms stand up to hear about how these people didn't let their pain stop them. They had a race to run. We tend to think of life as climbing a ladder. The better we're doing or more blessed it seems like we are, the higher on the ladder we go. I'm not sure exactly what we think will be at the top of this ladder, but we're bound and determined to climb it until we find out. This is great imagery when life is going well, but when we face a setback, unexpected pain, or times of failure, it feels like we slip and completely fall off the ladder. We're back at the ground level looking up. Our hearts begin to sink as we look up and realize that we're starting at square one again. The good thing is, we don't have to look at life like this. It's actually a pretty inaccurate way to look at the seasons of life that we face.

We aren't climbing a ladder; we're running a race. Sure, we find ourselves in difficult times and painful obstacles, but these are merely trips and falls that we can get up from along the way. We're not left on our backs wondering if it's even worth it to start climbing again. We are down for a moment, but we can start the race again exactly where we fell. Getting back up simply takes heart, determination, and of course some help. The kind of heart and strength that we need in order to make it through our pain and our setbacks comes from truly knowing who God is. Has someone ever come along and helped you back to your feet after you fell down? The truth is, you have a Father who is there beside you and will always stretch out His hand to help pick you up when you're down. He wants to help you, and He wants to run this race with you, even if it makes Him breathe heavy and leaves Him with aching sides. That's right, you'd be surprised how much of your pain is also God's pain, but you'd be even more surprised to find out how He loves you so much that He will run next to you and go through every single fall with you along the way.

I used to work at a physical rehabilitation hospital, and I saw many people who were fighting for the chance to get their strength back. For some, they just needed to gain their strength and endurance back in order to be able to do everyday activities normally again. For others, it was a struggle to move or speak. Even in what seemed to be their lowest points, many of the people around me knew their purpose, and they knew it wasn't to be stuck there. There's absolute beauty in healing. The process of healing may seem grueling or rigorous, but there is so much inspiration in watching someone be healed. This unexplainable swell of emotions and spirit seem to rise in our chest when we see someone beat the odds placed against them and live out their purpose once more. I think even the pain has a purpose. A sting of pain can highlight an enormous amount of strength. God doesn't place this kind of pain on us. He loves us as His children and always wants the best for us, but He can always use the pain that we go through for ways of good.

And we know that in all things God works for the good of those who love him, who have been called according to his purpose.
Romans 8:28 NIV

God is not the source of our pain, but He is the source of our strength through our pain. He is the one who can take our painful stories and make them ever so beautiful. He is the one who designed us to feel awe, wonder, and inspiration at the thought of healing. God is an incredible storyteller who can take the worst of situations and work them for stunning tales of strength, trust, and love. Even in your times of pain, you can trust that your Heavenly Father is there with you giving you strength and the power to get back up. He cares about you so much, and when He sees His child hurting, it breaks His heart. God wants to use your pain for good. When you fall, He's there to put a band aid on you and tell you that everything is going to be okay. You simply have to trust Him.

When God places a band aid on our cuts and scrapes, it usually looks different than what we expect. His band aid for us could look like a comforting friend. His band aid for us could look like an anonymous gift. His band aids look like "I love you" and "Let's get coffee. I miss you."

Do you remember the kids' band aids that
would come in all sorts of colorful designs
and patterns? When we grow up, we tend to
ditch those and go for the more bland, beige
ones, but I think God loves healing us
through colorful, childlike people and
situations that lift us when we're down.
Next time you've fallen down, don't look for
the beige around you. Allow yourself to be
healed in all of the colorful ways that God
delights in.

About a year ago, I flew on a plane for the first time in my life. I'd like to say that I was super cool about it, but the whole experience was kind of terrifying. For starters, I quickly found out that airports are not my scene. I'm not the world's greatest at adapting to new environments quickly. Side note, if there's ever a zombie apocalypse, you probably shouldn't pick me to be on your team of survivors. Anyway. I'm not a huge fan of the hustle and bustle of airport life, and I'm even less of a fan of prices for airport food. Being on the plane is another beast in itself. Taking off had an interesting effect on my body. I remember being so nervous about all the shaking of the plane, and then as we ascended higher and higher, my head felt lighter and lighter. It'd be my luck to pass out right there in front of God and everyone. I wasn't as concerned about my health from passing out as I was with how lame I would look to the people around me, ya know?

Several hours later, I found myself getting off of the plane completely fine and almost fully conscious. I stumbled into the big city of Orlando, Florida for a weeklong work trip. Yep, work. I was spending the week with a group of about ten people from my hometown in Arkansas to work for a business convention. I'm not really sure if I can say what company we were working for. (It was Microsoft.) We were with a team of hundreds of under qualified and over jet lagged employees helping to be the face of this convention for about twenty thousand attendees. Lots of people, lots of noise. Again, this wasn't quite my scene. I spent that week working twelve hour to sixteen hour shifts every day, and then I got to enjoy another adventure of packing up and flying back home. "Tired" is an understatement for the way that I felt by the time the trip was over.

I say all of that to get to my real point here. I left for that trip ready to get away from home and to experience whatever Orlando threw my way. I was excited and nervous to fly for the first time, and I had hopeful expectations of what that week would hold. That week held so many wonderful, culture shocking, crazy, top of the world, and bottom of the sea memories for me, but what I remember the most is the feeling I had when I returned back home. As

I started driving from the airport back into familiar neighborhoods and cooler, crisp air, an overwhelming feeling of joy and belonging overcame me. Home never looked so beautiful.

"When he came to his senses, he said, 'How many of my father's hired servants have food to spare, and here I am starving to death! I will set out and go back to my father and say to him: Father, I have sinned against heaven and against you. I am no longer worthy to be called your son; make me like one of your hired servants.' So he got up and went to his father.."
Luke 15:17-20 NIV

I think most of us have felt homesick at some point in our lives. There's an inner longing in all of us to have somewhere to call home. Maybe you think of home as the town where you grew up, or perhaps your dream home is somewhere on the beach. I have a dream of living in a small cabin in the mountains someday, surrounded by creation and a family to pour love into. All of us have a unique sense of home, but we are also prone to wander and want more. We find ourselves reaching a point in life where we always dreamed to be, being surrounded by the things we've only delighted our imaginations with for years, and yet there's still more. The inner longing doesn't go away quite like we thought it would. This is because we're looking for a sense of being home in all the wrong ways.

Home is so much more than a place; it's a person. Home is being in the Father's arms. Whether we recognize it or not, we're all designed to yearn for the times we can merely be with our loving Father. Other things, people, and places can make us feel wonderful for a while, but true and lasting satisfaction comes from being with God. Luckily for us, we don't have to pack up all our bags or travel the world in order to be with Him. God is with us wherever we go. He has an amazing way of bringing home to us. When we feel like we don't have a home, God is there. When we feel like we don't belong, we belong to Him. When we feel completely alone, He is right next to us, caring for us and loving us.

In the story of the prodigal son, we see a young man who is desperate to get away from his father. He wants to live his life doing anything that he wants, wherever he wants. Then something incredible happens. This son who wanted nothing to do with his father starts realizing how badly he wants to be back in that love and care. The way he imagined his life without his dad didn't go at all how he had planned. Even when this young man was in the worst of situations, he knew that he could run back to his father. That's where his heart longed to be. That's where your heart and my heart still long to be. Deep down, in the midst of our messiness, we long to run to a father who will care for us just as we are. When we feel weak, dirty, or all used up, the best thing for our souls is to know God's love for us enough to be confident to run to Him for care.

But while he was still a long way off, his father saw him and was filled with compassion for him; he ran to his son, threw his arms around him and kissed him.
Luke 15:20 NIV

The love of God looks like a father running toward his broken son. The moments when we feel like we should run away from God are actually the moments that we need to run toward Him the most. When we find ourselves down in the dumps, ashamed of where we are and what we've done, we can be confident that we have a Father that loves us so much He would run toward us even after our failures. If you take one step back toward God, He will sprint the rest of the way to meet you. That's the love He has for you. God cares so much more about the one step that you take toward Him than He does about the thousand you took away from Him. He's not mad at you. He's not waiting to punish you. God is waiting for you to turn around just enough to see Him running after you. He wants you to feel His arms around you and experience the compassion that He has for you. This is home.

Our home is with God. This is the place where our wounds can heal, and our hearts can soar. Being with Him gives us the strength and refreshment that we truly need. God gives us a safe place to completely be ourselves with him. When we're joyful and excited for the future, He is there celebrating with us. When we're broken and can't imagine the thought of facing the world another day, He is there pouring His compassion and care onto us. The funny thing about the prodigal son story is that even though the son made the first move to come back to the father, it was the father who saw the son first. The father saw the son before the son ever even looked up at him. When we're in a state of shame, guilt, loneliness, or anything else that makes us feel separated from God, it makes it hard to look up. All we see is the ground in front of us, and we don't even realize that God already has his eyes set on us.

God sees you. He is actively looking for you when you feel lost. There will never be a time that your Heavenly Father forgets about you. Even if you don't see Him there, I promise He has already seen you. God sees you when you're a long way off, and He overflows with compassion and love for you. Nothing can take that away, and nothing can replace that true feeling of being home with Him. If you feel lost, come home.

When I was in sixth grade, the swing set was officially dubbed the "cool spot." If you wanted any chance at making it to an open swing, you had to finish your lunch at lightning speed and full sprint to the playground before anyone else could get there. Who would've thought that getting to the swing set would become a choking hazard? Once you made it to an open swing, it was like sitting on a golden throne that had been sculpted just for that glorious moment. Kings of nations haven't felt that kind of achievement. This was the closest thing to pure bliss that a kid could feel at that time. If you've never experienced this feeling, I strongly recommend you get a few of your closest friends together and try it sometime.

Let's lay out some facts here. Being in the sixth grade is stressful. Catching the bus, pop quizzes, hoping your mom packed something good for lunch. The weight of the world is on your shoulders when you become the big dog on campus. We needed the swing set. It was like our island vacation for thirty minutes of the day. For me, it was the place where I could be surrounded by my friends and forget the worries of the classroom. We had a blast seeing how high we could swing or trying to flip out of the seat when we got as high as we could. Sure, it might be dangerous, but that's life. As time went on, we found different variations of games that we could play on the swings. We could play swing tag, or we could play catch as we were soaring through the air. Eventually, we found ourselves at swing dodgeball.

This was undoubtedly the most fun game that we had come up with... for a while. It started off so exhilarating trying to duck and dodge while swinging through the air. If you were throwing, you got the thrill of strategizing the ways you would eliminate your opponents. After a while, it became kind of aggressive though. Kids weren't just tossing the ball at each other and laughing as they played together. Kids were pelting each other with this ball and sometimes really getting hurt. I'll never forget a friend I had named Caleb who got hit so hard with the ball that he flipped out of his seat, landing face first on the ground. It had gotten ruthless.

When did we stop playing with each other and start aiming for each other? I don't mean just on the swing set; I mean in life. It seems as though when we grow older, we stop seeing people around us as friends we can play with and start seeing them instead as targets that we should be aiming for. What would it look like if we stopped letting comparison eat away at something that was supposed to be innocent? Our hearts weren't designed to handle the capacity of comparison that we live with today. Our souls certainly weren't designed to look at God's creation and make enemies out of them. Maybe we were actually made to stop and play.

"Peace I leave with you, My peace I give to you; not as the world gives do I give to you. Let not your heart be troubled, neither let it be afraid."
John 14:27 NKJV

The world can never give us the peace that we so long for. Only Jesus can. We often strive for achievement and excellence in order to fill the void that actually needs peace. If you didn't feel like you were under constant pressure to produce, who would you be? If you could fill that spot in your heart that is desperately crying out for peace, you would look like a completely new person. In order to fill that spot, we need Jesus.

Jesus is a shining example of someone who lived with extraordinary peace despite His circumstances. He knew who He was and whose He was. Jesus had similar pressures that we feel today. He was expected to be a great king who would come and take the world by storm, overthrowing powers and governments in order to free His people. When He showed up as a poor carpenter boy, can you imagine the disappointment and disbelief He faced from others? He never lived up to that dream that those people were hoping for; thankfully, He lived up to so much more. Jesus had such a close connection to the Father, and His entire identity surrounded that relationship. When I feel like peace is too far gone and my self-worth is dependent on where I am in life compared to other people, it's a good indicator that I'm not placing my identity in who my Father says I am. In searching for what your identity is, there are a few things that we can conclude that your identity is not.

Your identity is not in your sins. When the Father looks down at you, He beams with joy over His beautiful creation. God doesn't see us for our sin. He sees us in our most pure form, and He yearns to protect His creation from the harm of sin. He put on skin and bone and gave His life for us just to be able to protect us from the sting of sin. He cares for us that greatly and sees us as that worthy. Your sin shouldn't build a wall between you and God. He forgave you long ago. In the midst of your sin, allow God to see you and take care of you. Allow His forgiveness to cleanse you and bring you closer to Him.

Your identity is not in your accomplishments. You do not have to compete and strive to be who God created you to be. He created you to be loved by Him. There's no amount of work that you have to do for that. You simply accept the love that He gives you. We don't deserve God's kind of radical, unwavering love, and everything in our nature wants to push back and say that we can't accept it because we don't deserve it. When you finally choose to accept it, though, you feel surrounded by an indescribable wave of belonging. You can finally feel like you. This is who you were made to be and how you were created to live. In the center of His love.

So we do not lose heart. Though our outer self is wasting away, our inner self is being renewed day by day.
2 Corinthians 4:16 ESV

It's easy to let the world bring us down if we don't keep sight of who God is and who He says we are. We tend to lose heart when a business deal goes wrong, when a loved one passes, or when we feel like we've failed those who are close to us.

When things feel broken, let God fix them. The weight of the world has been taken off your shoulders. Run free knowing the pressure is off of you. Be that shining light that God has called you to be and know that you can rest in His goodness. Every single new day is another chance for us to be renewed and drawn closer to our Father who loves us so very much. He's proud of who you are, just as you are, and He will forever want the best for you.

⮩

Fall is beginning here in Arkansas, and today was one of the first days for cooler air to wash over this area. I absolutely adore the feeling of a cool breeze brushing against my face, so I decided to go for a drive with the windows down… blasting music that reminded me of my childhood, of course. There's something incredible and almost therapeutic that happens when you let the windows down and sing as loud as you can to songs that make you feel like a kid again. Allowing the setting sun to warm your cheeks as old neighborhoods are filled with the sound of your voice belting out old rock songs can make you feel free. At that moment, I wasn't thinking about what the rest of my schedule held. I wasn't even thinking about everything from earlier in the day. I was just right there right then. I was present in the moment, allowing myself to simply be.

There's nothing extraordinary about this story, but there is something wonderfully magical about the feeling of it all. There's a real sense of peace, purpose, and belonging that comes from taking a step away from the demands of the world. In the Bible, Jesus went away on His own a lot to talk to the Father. I imagine He got a similar feeling when He was doing that. He wasn't planning out the rest of His day or worrying about a business meeting that afternoon. He was letting the windows down and simply spending that moment with God, not doing, but being. This is where true refreshment comes from. When we can be ourselves with God and not place the weight of expectation on our shoulders, we find peace and joy that we can't explain.

Maybe you need to go for a drive. Roll the windows down, listen to creation around you, blast some music, and talk to God. Let it all out. Be yourself. Allow yourself to be loved and to feel peace in that moment. The more time you can find to stop producing and start being, the more you will experience the peace of God that passes all understanding, and you will begin the beautiful process of loving the person that God has created you to be. In an equally marvelous way, you will begin loving other people for who they are, right where they are. You'll allow yourself to take your expectations from them, and you'll no longer need criteria for loving others. You will love them because you know what it feels like to be loved for who you are. What a beautiful feeling we get to share. Go take that car ride. Go swing on that swing set. Go allow yourself to breathe and be loved by the One who knows you best.

There's nothing quite like catching up with an old friend. So many stories are told, laughs are shared, and connection is sparked. I have certain friends in my life who I try to catch up with every few months or so, and I'm always amazed at how much the friendship still feels natural. There are no awkward silences or icebreakers needed. There's just the warm connection of friends who have been waiting to see each other one day and the wonderful fulfillment of being together.

Coffee shops are my favorite place to meet up with old friends. The atmosphere allows for hours of talking and being relaxed together. Sometimes the conversations are very nostalgic as we reminisce about the past and everything that has brought us to that moment. Other times we turn back into kids and let out our fiery passion for what we want to do with our lives. Dreams are shared, inspiration is drawn from each other, and a sense of wonder and excitement for the future lingers in the air. I love these conversations and the emotions that arise when being with a friend that I've missed so much. I think there's something necessary to it. I think we all need to be reminded every once in a while that we have people who care for us and who we can connect with, even if we haven't seen them in a while. That's the beauty of true relationships. We can have someone on our side even when we don't realize it.

That same day two of Jesus' disciples were going to the village of Emmaus, which was about seven miles from Jerusalem. As they were talking and thinking about what had happened, Jesus came near and started walking along beside them. But they did not know who he was.
Luke 24:13-16 CEV

It's so easy to become blind to the people next to us who care so much for us. When our problems feel too big, people can feel too far away. Life happens, and we all have an inept ability to fill our schedules with more projects, more deadlines, and more stress but at the same time lessen the value of simply being around more people. We need friends who can come and walk along beside us, and we have a perfect friend who is always with us, even when we don't know who He is. Jesus is a perfect friend, and He wants you to surround yourself with other great friends who can walk through life right next to you. The right people can keep you grounded when you need it, and they can also lift you up and dare you to aim for the stars. He knows you need that kind of connection, even when you try with all your might to stay away from it.

Why do we avoid connection so much? There are so many healthy things for our souls that come from connection with Jesus and with others, yet we seem timid to step out and let ourselves be truly deep and truly us with people. It's not a complicated answer to the question. It's scary. We've all had friendships that have ended badly or relationships that left us scarred. We have wounds in our hearts that we've pacified for years, but we've never allowed them to be healed. Our pain is rooted in past relationships, but our healing comes from the right relationships. Jesus wants to heal that pain inside of you that keeps you from connecting with people. He wants to come along beside you, no matter where you're at, and walk with you through whatever you're facing. He's a good friend.

Maybe you've never thought of Jesus as a "friend" before. We always hear the He is the Lord of all, the King of Kings, and the Son of God. He is indeed all of these things, but how much would it change your relationship with Him if you saw Jesus as your absolute best friend? I'm positive it would make it easier to connect with Him, and you may even start seeing Him in places where you never recognized Him before. He's been walking along side you this whole time. You just have to see Him for who He is. Jesus cares for you and wants to go on this journey with you, as your friend. There are paths we've all been down where we didn't see Jesus anywhere. We were walking down a long road, and even if we had seen a glimpse of Him, we sure didn't recognize it as that. It's been Him the whole time. In the long walks and in the darkest hours, Jesus has been by our side.

❧

"Friend" may be the title that some of us actually need for God. It's hard to look at God as a perfect father when you've always had a horrible one on this side of Heaven. Even the term "good father" seems to be abstract for a lot of us. There are so many who have never even come close to experiencing the goodness of a father, and God choosing that image can seem daunting and even taunting. If you can't see God as a father, see Him as a friend. God can be exactly who you need Him to be, because He is already exactly what you need. If you need a friend, He will be there to walk with you. If you need a counselor, He's a wonderful one. If you need a comforter, He will provide a peace that passes all our understanding.

Don't let the fear of your earthly father keep you from having a connection with your Heavenly one. If a father scares you, let Him be your friend. Let Him walk with you, side by side, through all of your ups and downs. It's the connection that your heart longs for and your soul needs. It can be scary, but perfect love casts out fear. God wants to heal your wounds and open up your capacity to trust again. Once He does that with your relationship with Him, it's marvelous what He can open up in your relationships with others. You have more friends on your side than you think; you just might need to catch up with them a little bit.

When you can start seeing Jesus by your side in everything that you do, it creates a confidence and reassurance in your heart that everything is going to work out for good. He has a good way of bringing out our joy and our boldness. When we can't muster it up ourselves, He gives us His strength. Have you ever talked to a friend who was so filled with joy and had such huge dreams that it rubbed off on you? We can't help it when we're around certain people. Even on our worst days, we spend time around that one friend who always knows how to pick us up when we're down and make us laugh, and we can't help but leave the conversation a little bit more like them. The light and joy that they carry is so strong that it can also light us up. This is what a friendship with Jesus looks like.

After Jesus sat down to eat, he took some bread. He blessed it and broke it. Then he gave it to them. At once they knew who he was, but he disappeared. They said to each other, "When he talked with us along the road and explained the Scriptures to us, didn't it warm our hearts?"
Luke 24:30-32 CEV

"Didn't it warm our hearts?" It may take a while to see Jesus for who He actually is, but once we do, our hearts are warmed. We start to realize that we were never alone on that long road. We never had to face any of those trials by ourselves. Jesus was walking alongside us the whole time. The tone of our whole lives changes when we see Jesus for who He is: our friend. He walks with us and talks to us. He's not far off just waiting to see if we'll make the right or wrong move. He's in it with us. Jesus loves guiding us and bringing us joy. All we have to do is allow Him to.

Jesus isn't selfish. He doesn't want to be our only friend. He will bring so many other people into our lives who He can use to help us grow and learn. I have friends in my life that I know are from Jesus because when I'm with them, I start learning how to trust more and dream bigger again. I have friends who I know Jesus gave me because they're head over heels for Jesus themselves, and they are never too selfish to keep that joy from me. So many people have shown me what Jesus looks like, and they are the greatest friends that I've ever had. Surround yourself with people who remind you of Jesus. There are people in this life who will love you more than you deserve, push you farther than you can go, and bring guidance to so much healing in your life. Jesus is at the centerpiece of this friend group, and He wants it to be as big as possible.

If you need a friend, you always have a perfect one to reach out to. He will never let you down or hurt you. It's not in His nature. He's the best friend that we could ever ask for, and He's the one that we have always needed. You might not be able to see Him at first, but He's right there walking with you, side by side.

Throughout my life, I've found that the simplest conversations have had the most profound impact on me. Talks about love, life, feelings, and the things that connect all of us seem to give life to me. I know what you're thinking. "Those kinds of talks aren't simple at all!" The truth is these things can be simple if we allow them to be. Love, for example, is pretty simple, but it's actually us who make it complicated. Love looks like reaching out to someone in need. Love looks like baking fresh, rising cookies with those that you adore and laughing at how burnt the bottoms turned out. Love can show itself in so many different small moments of our daily lives, and if we allow ourselves, we can see love even in the small questions like, "How was your day?"

It sparks a kind of joy in all of us when we're seen. More than just being looked at, but when we're truly seen for who we are. It lifts us up when somebody actually notices that we are going through a tough time or that we have a little bit of extra joy than usual shimmering in our eyes. When we are noticed, and when we feel like we belong, it unlocks something in our hearts that allows us to love and receive love in a higher capacity than before. It's when we feel invisible that we start to slip into seasons of life that feel a bit more cold than usual. Luckily for us, we are always seen. Not in a creepy way, but we're seen through a lens of deep love and compassion. The real us, everything that we feel and are on the inside, is seen by our Father and is eternally cared for. God obviously cares about the "big" things in our lives, but what we often forget is that He cares about every one of the small things too. I think one of God's favorite things to do is talk to us and ask us how our day was.

God probably doesn't want to hear our typical after school answer. You know the one. When a parent asks their child, "How was school today?" and they are met with the infamous, "Good." Yeah, that answer. Our heavenly Father is looking for something quite a bit deeper than that. He cares for us so much that He wants to hear the details and all of the ups and downs we felt throughout the day. More than caring about the day itself, God cares about how the day had an effect on our souls. We could almost switch the phrasing of the question, "How was your day?" to something more like, "How did today affect your soul?" All of sudden, we find ourselves actually having to think about the answer to the question. Was today really that bad if you got to experience God's peace and presence through all of the things that you faced? Was today really that good if you forgot to let yourself experience love and share it with someone else? We are surrounded by so many urgent needs each day that it's easy to forget what is important. Love is what matters. Being loved and giving love can transform the darkest of nights into the brightest of days. So, how was your day?

When I was little, visiting my grandparents' house was better than visiting Disneyworld. It was a magical feeling turning onto their drive and catching the first glimpse of their little brick home. The enormous sycamore tree in the front yard served as the welcome committee as we eagerly leapt out of the car to see grandma and grandpa. On warm summer days, you could easily catch me in the backyard running around and playing with my grandparents' hound dog, Spot, or being amazed at various kinds of birds that chose to wash in the bird bath. On winter days, we'd be cozied up inside the house watching movies and drinking soothing drinks that warm a person's soul. While the place itself does hold a special place in my heart, it's the family and the memories made there that really resonate in my heart. Some memories you just never forget.

The biggest tradition that I remember for myself was hanging out in Grandpa's room. Most days, immediately after I entered through the front door and crossed the saloon doors that lead to the kitchen, my grandpa and I would load up on snacks and proudly make our way to the back bedroom. We would spend hours back there eating, laughing, watching television, and lying on the bed with our hands rested behind our heads. If you paid close enough attention, you could catch us sneaking back in the kitchen to retrieve a few cold drinks again before making our way back to our little piece of Heaven. I'm not entirely sure who looked forward to this time more, me or my grandpa. The excitement, love, and childlike wonder was fairly equal on both sides.

I picture spending time with God a lot like spending time with my grandpa. There's no fear or formality to it at all. This kind of quality time stems from love and the joy of getting to be together. Laughter, tears, and even silence are all welcomed with open arms. Talking to God and spending time with Him should feel like being a kid resting in the presence of someone who loves you more than you can imagine. While God may not fill us up with candy or soda, He will fill our souls up with joy and our hearts up with love. Seeing God for who He really is and truly connecting with Him will give us that special feeling of never wanting the moments with Him to end. He doesn't want them to end either.

When I remember you upon my bed, and meditate on you in the watches of the night; for you have been my help, and in the shadow of your wings I will sing for joy. My soul clings to you; your right hand upholds me.
Psalm 63:6-8 ESV

Like a child that clings onto the shirt of their grandparent because they never want that goodbye hug to end, our souls should cling to God. If only we accepted how much He loves us, we would cling ever so tightly to His very presence in our lives. This isn't a kind of love that depends on our performance or merit. It's a kind of love that completely stuns us in our tracks and allows us to quit performing and start being utterly ourselves in the presence of our Heavenly Father. It may catch us off guard at first, but we will quickly find ourselves running with childlike eagerness and joy into the presence (that back bedroom) of God.

It's a true gift to be able to open our whole hearts to God. Allowing Him into our spaces of joy, excitement, grief, regret, and everything in between can drastically change the way we communicate with Him and spend our time with Him. Humans have always had a hard time staying consistent in communicating with God. We use the word "discipline" to describe our prayer lives. Do you want to know why that is? Our prayer lives suffer when we have a misconception of who God is. It's hard to make time every day to pray to a God who sees our guilt and shame the same way we see our guilt and shame. It's scary to approach a God who is angry at us for our sin or disappointed in us because of our shortcomings. But God doesn't see us this way. He genuinely views us as His children, and He could not be more in love with us. Not just the parts of us that behave correctly. Not just the parts of us that we bring to church on Sunday mornings. God loves every part of us. He loves the good, the bad, and the ugly. There's absolutely nothing that I could have done at five years old to earn or deserve the love of my grandpa. I'm pretty sure I couldn't even spell my full name correctly at that point. But there is one thing that I'm sure of: his love for me was unwavering, and the exact same can be said about our Father in Heaven.

God wants us to run into His arms with confidence and assurance of His love. We don't need to be timid around Him or feel the need to hide things about ourselves that we don't think are good. He just wants us. He loves to be with us. He left Heaven just to be among us and bring us closer to Him. That doesn't sound like a God who's hard to talk to or terrifying to be around. He sounds like our one true source of love, no matter what, because He is.

God loved us far before we even had the ability to love back. He loved us before any of the choices we've made and before any of the paths we've gone down in life. Our steps don't determine His love. In fact, it's quite the opposite. God's love is often the driving force of what guides our steps. It was the love that my grandpa had for me that guided my small footsteps down the hallway behind him. Yes, I loved him with everything in me, but he loved me first. It was his love that sparked my heart back in response. The love of God flowed through my grandpa in ways that I wouldn't understand for many years after. It's gentleness and tenderness that bring us close to our Creator. It's His complete care for us that makes us feel safe enough to soften our hearts toward Him and allow Him into our lives. The weight is never on our shoulders. The only thing we should feel is His presence lifting us up when we can't lift ourselves up. We can't live this life isolated, even on our best days. We need a God who is always here for us, providing perfect care for us. And we have one. God will always be there for you, ready to ask you, "How was your day?"

A lot of my elementary and junior high school years were spent around the same group of guys. One of my best friends in the world was the grandson of our elementary school's superintendent, so of course, we scored some special treatment. We could always count on ending our days in her office sneaking special treats and then hitting the playground for an hour or so before having to depart home. This was our after-school tradition for years. Even after moving up into the big bad world of junior high school, we managed to find a bus that let off right in the parking lot of our old elementary school. We didn't give up our snacks and play time that easily. Some days, there would be one or two of us hanging out on the playground throwing rocks and talking about life. Other days, we'd have a whole gang with us ready to start a pickup basketball game or jump off of slides that were way too tall. If you were scared of heights, you would be volunteered as the first person to jump off. That's just how the cookie crumbles.

One day after school, we all met up on the playground, per usual, but we had a very important agenda on our minds. We were all planning on staying the night at our buddy Poarch's house for his birthday. His first name is Andrew, but you'd never know it if you hung around us because his last name was way too cool to ever use his first name. We've all had that friend at some point. The plan was to go home, pack up a night's worth of belongings (which in the seventh grade usually fit inside of a plastic Walmart bag), and meet back up at Poarch's house. After packing up as quick as possible, we all made it back to his house for dinner, birthday cake, presents, and games. His house was like a second home. It's one of those places where you naturally feel like you belong, and you're welcomed.

As the night moved on, our minds began to craft plans on how we could spend the rest of this birthday evening. Now, me and my buddies were never known for our great decision making. We weren't spending our days running wild and getting the cops called on us, but nonetheless, we were teenage boys. Intuition was nonexistent at this point. But bad decisions usually make for good stories, so here's a great one. A few blocks away from Poarch's house was a wooded area with plenty of trails to explore. Sounds great, right? Wrong. It turns out that the only way we could get up to this wooded area was to climb up what was called "Suicide Hill." Yes, that's truly the name of this hill, and you bet, we decided we were going to climb it. At night. In the rain. Still pumped up on a chocolate cake high, we threw on our jackets and made our way up the street. After a few minutes of walking through the neighborhood, we found ourselves at the base of Suicide Hill. We didn't know exactly where we were going, but we knew the general direction was up, so up we went.

In the cold, wet night, we started our ascent through mud, rocks, and shrubs on the way up. It didn't take long to realize why this hill gained the name that it did. To this day, it's probably the steepest climb I have ever made. Very rarely do I ever find myself climbing on all fours just to go forward, but that was where all of us found ourselves most of that climb. We were clinging on to rocks and giving each other tips and tricks on how to get past certain tough areas. A friend of mine fell on his butt harder than I've seen anyone else fall, and us being guys, laughed pretty hard for a while. I remember points on the trail when I was holding on to vines with thorns on them just to pull myself up. We were wet, bruised, dirty, and exhausted by the time we made it to the top. It was awesome. It wasn't something that was planned, and it certainly wasn't something that was easy. It was an experience that's incredibly rememberable, though.

The funny thing is that I know we took an easier way down, but that's not the part that I can remember. I couldn't' tell you a good story about our easy trip back down to the house, but I'll never forget the way up. I think this happens to all of us throughout our lifetimes. We find ourselves in the middle of the hardest climbs of our lives, and at the moment, we're not even sure what's going to be at the top. We're slipping and falling, and we're grasping for anything that will help us get to where we want to be. Sometimes we're the friend that's trying to help someone else get past the hard spots, and sometimes we're the one that just landed straight on our butt. These are the moments we tend to remember, though. When things are easy and comfortable, they also quickly become stale and forgettable. A lot of life happens on the climb. When we go off the beaten path and find ourselves in uncomfortable territory, we remember these moments and the lessons they teach for the rest of our lives. It can be difficult and ugly on the way up, but it's never impossible to reach where we're going.

"I have told you these things, so that in me you may have peace. In this world you will

Life never seems to go quite as we planned it. If it were up to me, I would plan out a quiet life where struggles and worries were nothing but an imagination. I'd also be surrounded by an endless amount of coffee and puppies. Unfortunately, this isn't what life looks like. Our journeys are full of unforeseen twists and turns, but even when we're not sure what the path ahead looks like, we must trust that there's someone who does. We may not know where the path less traveled will take us, but we have a best friend who will never leave us that knows every single step. Jesus doesn't promise us that it will be easy, but He gives us peace through the journey. He has already overcome what we can't, and He loves us so much that He guides us and strengthens us along the way. We are never expected to make the climb alone, and we can have peace even when we know that hardship lies ahead of us.

Sometimes, all we need is to know that we're not alone. Knowing that we have someone with us often helps us continue to move forward. It gives us peace and security. We weren't meant to be alone, and Jesus knows that we need Him with us in the hard moments. It's in the not-so-pretty moments of life where the peace and grace

of Jesus shines through the brightest.
These moments, or even seasons, give us
the opportunity to feel a kind of joy that
doesn't typically make sense. When my
friends and I were falling down and getting
bruised up, it would have been easy to get
frustrated or discouraged, but that's not
what happened. We laughed. We enjoyed
the immensely hard climb up because we
were together. Being with someone, with a
friend, can turn the hardest of situations
into something enjoyable. Good company
brings peace, and Jesus keeps us perfect
company.

Being alone is a scary thought. It's in
the loneliness that our battles feel much,
much harder to fight. When we're alone, we
spend time thinking about our past failures
or how we're not strong enough to live a life
worth living. Loneliness breeds deception.
Being alone makes life so much more
difficult to navigate because we weren't
created to be alone. We were created to be
in relationship. Our souls feel more at home
when we live in relationship with our
Heavenly Father and with one another.
Laughter turns so much sweeter when we
can share it with others, and tears can be
wiped away by caring hands. If you get
overwhelmed at the thought of being alone,
guess what... you're not alone. We all desire
to have someone to pull us up when we're
down. We all long to be seen, loved, and

valued. Our hearts need this, and God knows this.

Jesus promised us that we would never have to be alone. His spirit rests in us forever, and not only does it rest in us, but it *helps* us. In everything that we go through, we have a helper. We have an advocate working on our behalf when we can't work for ourselves. The lonely moments never have to scare us again because God loves us so much that He gave His Spirit to us in order to make sure we never feel alone again. The lengths that our Father has taken to make sure we don't go through this life alone are amazing. He created friends and loved ones to be around us. He sent His one and only son to live with us and die for us. He sent his Spirit of truth to remain with us forever. God loves you so much and reaches out for you time and time again to remind you that you're not alone. He sees you no matter where you are, and He places Himself right there with you.

It's easy to recognize God's presence when it feels like a hand pulling us up, but it's equally as easy to dismiss His presence when it feels like we're clinging to a thorn bush. During my young hiking experience, it was incredibly easy to see I was being helped out when my friends were grabbing my hand and pulling me up. It was a lot harder to see that the thorn bush I pulled myself up on was helping me too. Sometimes being pulled out of our low points hurts. It feels like it would be easier just to fall back. We already know what it was like at the bottom, but now it's a painful climb up. And then we find ourselves in a peculiar position. Halfway up a steep mountain, clinging to thorns. It's painful to be pulled up, and it's not quite the kind of help that we were counting on, but it's the help that has been placed perfectly in our path. We don't always get to choose what our help looks like; we just have to choose whether or not we'll accept it. Are you going to let God help pull you up even when it's painful? I promise that the pain of the climb is so much better than the sting of the fall.

Today, choose to keep climbing. Remember that you're not alone, and God has perfectly placed Himself within your reach. You can pull yourself up through His strength, and you can lean on Him for support. When the path you're on doesn't look like the path you've planned, trust that He is still leading you. God is with you even when you go off the beaten path.

During my senior year of high school, my friends and I had a tradition of playing late night hide and seek. By late night, I mean technically tomorrow morning. Three in the morning was our sweet spot for some reason. Walmart was apparently also our sweet spot for some reason, so we'd make our way to wally world and borderline break the law for a couple of hours. I think once you pass a certain time of night, you can actually get away with anything inside of a Walmart. Don't quote me on that, though. Anyway, our hiding spots would range from the Christmas decoration area to the diapers and strollers. If you were really bold, you would stay on the move or hide in plain sight. Even though we were probably the most suspicious group of kids to ever step foot into that store, they luckily never put any signs up of us or asked for a bounty on us.

During one intense game in particular, I made the genius decision to hide inside of a clothes rack. You know, one of those circular ones with all the shirts hanging around it. As I was sitting in my perfectly designed hiding spot scoffing at how much smarter I was than everyone else, something very terrible happened. An employee decided to make camp right next to me. Like, directly beside where I was sitting. During the next hour or so, I felt as if the rest of the world was going to have to go on without me. I was quickly losing hope the longer it took this employee to stock clothes next to me. This may have been the exact moment that my prayer life started, too.

I eventually resorted to sending out SOS messages to my friends who, of course, did not come to get me. I had to make a move, and my bladder was telling me that I needed to act quickly. I pulled the coupe de gras of all maneuvers. I came to the conclusion that my best bet was to quietly (very quietly) slide my way out of the clothes rack on the opposite side of the employee and act like I had just been standing there looking at clothes. As if they would believe that I appeared out of thin air just to look at half priced women's shirts. This was my plan, and I was sticking to it.

I ended up making it out of that clothing rack without dying, but hiding seemed to get me into a situation that I would never want to be in. I didn't want to be seen, and it sent me into a very small place. We seem to grow up hiding just to play around, but then life seems to touch us in ways that make us want to truly hide. After experiencing some sort of pain or trauma, most of us have the natural instinct to hide. We don't want anyone to see us. Even if we're the center of attention, we don't allow people to see the real us. The real us has experienced loss that took something from us, and it can feel like we'll never get it back. The real us has done things that we can't share with everybody. The real us has been broken and bent, and it's much safer to hide than be denied.

Then the man and his wife heard the sound of the Lord God as he was walking in the garden in the cool of the day, and they hid from the Lord God among the trees of the garden. But the Lord God called to the man, "Where are you?" He answered, "I heard you in the garden, and I was afraid because I was naked; so I hid."
Genesis 3:8-10 NIV

Hiding stems from fear, and there's nothing scarier than being seen naked. I don't mean being physically naked but being vulnerable before others. Even being vulnerable before God. Letting someone into those places that most people have never seen can almost be paralyzing.

"If I'm denied for who I really am, maybe I'm not good enough to be known."

It's funny how we can be tricked into fear, but we must be convinced that we are loved. We don't run and hide when we feel truly loved, so why do we so often run and hide from our Father? Because it's hard to believe that He could really love us. We hide because we're afraid. We get this idea that God couldn't love us after the things that we've done or words that we've said to others. We even get the idea that God couldn't love us after the things it feels like He has put us through. It feels easier to hide than to go through any more pain. We feel more in control when we get to decide when we're seen. That's why we might let the Lord get a little peek of us right after we've gone to church, or we might inch closer to Him after we helped somebody else in need. Then as soon as we mess up or fall back into bad habits, we hide again. Our eyes stay focused on the ground instead of looking up to possibly face shame or judgment.

Maybe it's not God that you're hiding from. Maybe it's the people around you. If you've been outcasted before or been made to feel broken because of who you are, the last thing you want to do is open up again. It hurts the first time it happens, and it's not the kind of pain that we wish to endure again. We keep things surface level because at least those cuts don't go so deep. It's scary letting people know how hurt we've been, and it can be even more scary to allow people to see the things that make us shine. "What if they put my light out?"

Shine on. Even if your light has been dimmed down by the pain of the world, let it shine. All of us have been hurt, rejected, and let down. Every single one of us is carrying pain and burdens that the rest of the world may never see, but fear cannot be the navigator of our lives. Perfect love casts out fear, and love must take the driver's seat in our lives. Love allows your light to grow brighter, and love mends the wounds of what you've had to go through.

Love has a name, and His name is Jesus. It may seem too incredible to be true, but Jesus tenderly loves every single part of us. He loves our passions and our dreams, and He loves that parts of us that have been utterly smashed to pieces. He's not off put by any of the rejected parts of us. Our rejection makes us closer to Him.

People made fun of him, and even his friends left him. He was a man who suffered a lot of pain and sickness. We treated him like someone of no importance, like someone people will not even look at but turn away from in disgust. The fact is, it was our suffering he took on himself; he bore our

Jesus felt the pain of rejection. He was abandoned for simply being who He was. Jesus knows the pain of being turned away. Your pain is not yours to carry alone. None of us were created to hide. We were designed to be seen by others and by the perfect One who created us. Even though we tend to be terrified of letting ourselves be seen for who we really are, there's something created inside of us that still desires to be seen. We crave to be valued, loved, and accepted for who we are. All of us want to be good enough, and in the eyes of our Father, we are so much more than good enough. You're beautiful to Him. Every detail of you captivates Him. There is no part of your story that can ever turn God away from you, and it's when we recognize this level of love that we can begin to let our walls be chipped away. Only love can free us from the things that have made us hide for so long. Love rushes over us with the power to break the chains of shame, guilt, and fear. Love sees us.

You deserve to be seen. Your soul was beautifully orchestrated to be beheld and cherished. It can be terrifying, but it's worth taking the plunge. Allowing yourself to be vulnerable is so much more powerful than just covering up scars; it heals wounds. You may feel rejected by the world, but you are accepted by the King. In the moments when you want to shrivel up and bury yourself where nobody else can see you, remember you have a loving Father in Heaven who looks at you with nothing but love in His eyes. God's pretty good at supplying love for us that we can't supply for ourselves, and His love brings us closer and closer to Him with our arms open more and more.

Every part of you can be trusted with Him. The broken parts of you. The scared parts. The hurts, dreams, and passions inside. God has placed all of your passions inside of your heart for a reason, and He can use any part of your story for His glory. You deserve to be seen.

We started this journey being carried by our Father. We've felt His beaming smile looking down upon us as we experienced so many new things. He's taken us places we never imagined going, and He's made so many wonderful memories with us along the way. At the end of each day, though, there comes a time to go home. It's a refreshing constant that we have in our lives. Tired eyes and worn bones eventually lead us back to the place where we can find rest. We've ended this day at the park older than when we started, but God is still here to carry us back to the car and take us home.

It's beautiful that we often leave this life with the same dependence on God as when we entered it. I've worked with people in hospitals, churches, and homes that have reached a point in their lives where they require more help than they once needed. The Lord has sent people into their lives not only to help be their hands and feet, but He has sent them to also be His hands and feet. Even through the worst of situations, God is there to gently carry us from one life to the next, and He often uses people to help. Sometimes we don't want to leave the park. It's been such a beautiful walk with Him, and even through the highs and lows, we don't wish for it to end. We've been following our Father, though. He is good in all of His ways, and He never leads us astray. We know that we can trust His direction, even when He is guiding us home.

My sheep listen to my voice; I know them, and they follow me. I give them eternal life, and they shall never perish; no one will snatch them out of my hand. My Father, who has given them to me, is greater than all; no one can snatch them out of my Father's hand.
John 10:27-29 NIV

We will never slip out of the caring hands of our Father. No one can take us out of them either. He's always guiding us in our next steps, and we can always lean on Him and His understanding when the future seems unsure. The "park" of life is a beautiful place. People love, laugh, grow, reunite, play, cry, fall, and get back up here. Even when we get some scrapes on our knees and maybe drop an ice cream cone, we can look up at God at the end of the day and say it was so incredibly worth it. We can choose to walk back to the car sad and mourning that our time is over, or we can walk back to the car telling God how much fun we had and how we can't wait to get back home with Him and the rest of our family.

$$\backsim$$

It's easy to forget that we're not all in the same spot in our walks with God. I think that's where a lot of pain comes in when we have to watch someone that we love go home. It's easy to forget that they've already been the places that we've been, and they've made their own wonderful memories with the Father. We want to keep playing, but God knows that they need to go home with Him and get some rest. God has His first aid kit at home, and He can finally use it to take away any pain. God has a huge family at home, and He can finally add one more member to relish in it. God can tell bedtime stories of His glory at home, and He can make sure there's enough room for everyone to be comfortable. It's hard watching others get older and move on from their time in the park, but we can trust that God has them by the hand and is taking them to His beautiful home.

Questions and emotions seem to run everywhere during these times. There's nothing bad or wrong about either. All the questions that we have and all the emotions that we feel when a loved one passes can be comforted by the process of trusting God. Trust settles the raging questions in our minds, and trust extinguishes the rising flames of emotions that take over our hearts. Putting our trust in God can heal so many wounded areas of our souls. When you're having to watch a loved one go home, place your trust in a wonderful Father, and know that this isn't the end. It's just a change in scenery.

The unexpected hurts. We've all known people that have gone home too soon. It seems like they just started being able to play on their own, and now they're gone. It leaves an emptiness that compares to nothing else in the world. Most often, we're left with the question, "Why them?" These are the moments that seem the hardest to understand God's plan and His perspective of home. Rather than taking someone home, it feels like He just took them away. It doesn't feel fair. Even in these dark, dark storms, the only way to truly heal and find peace in our souls is to trust God. When we don't understand what He's doing, we have to lean on His understanding. We have to remember the truth about God. He is good. He is loving. He will never leave us nor forsake us. When we're in the mourning process, a lot of voices will try to tell us different things. Voices will try to challenge our view on God, but He always remains constant. God is walking through the storm with us.

> *Moses answered the people, "Do not be afraid. Stand firm and you will see the deliverance the Lord will bring you today. The Egyptians you see today you will never see again. The Lord will fight for you; you need only to be still."*
> *Exodus 14:13-14 NIV*

God is good when things are going good. But what is He when things seem like they're falling apart? God had taken the Israelites out of Egypt, completely away from their slavery and bondage. Walking with God was great when they were walking in freedom and confidence. Now they're facing a different situation, though. The Israelites are trapped between the raging waters of the sea and a vicious army chasing after them. There's no way out. They were given hope and a new life, just for it to seemingly be taken away again. This is what it feels like when we lose someone too soon and too young. Too innocent and too good for this world. It's like we got the miracle of their life, just for it to be taken away again. We were looking at freedom ahead, and now we're just looking at raging waters. In these moments, we have to trust what God has said to be true. He will fight for us. All we have to do is be still.

God split open the sea for the Israelites to walk through. Notice the way He led them. Through the storm. Even in the midst of what seems like the worst storm of our lives, God will lead us through it, and He will guide us the entire way to the other side. There is always another side. The storm doesn't last forever; neither does life on this side of Heaven. Everything comes back to God. We have to listen to His voice, take hold of His righteous right hand, and walk with Him through every journey life takes us on. There is always a light at the end of the tunnel, and our Father will always pick us up in His loving arms to take us somewhere new.

Goodbye for now.

What a beautiful journey life is. None of us could have expected that this is what it would be like, but it's more incredible that way. At one point, taking our first baby steps was the biggest adventure that we could imagine. Then one day, we find ourselves climbing the tallest trees and making so many friends along the way. We make mistakes. We end up hurting ourselves, and we may even hurt our friends and loved ones along the way but love always takes hold. Forgiveness allows us to flourish and grow even closer to each other, and it allows us to grow even closer to our Father. God is such a proud dad. He loves you just for being you. Nothing about your time at the park together surprises Him or makes him not want to take you home with Him. He loves you so very much, and while you're running around with your friends making new memories, He's right there on the park bench watching and radiating with joy. When you fall down, He comes running. He cares for your wounds, and He makes sure that you're strong enough to go play again. He loves you.

We all want different things out of life. We're wired and designed to have different goals and dreams. I think the one thing we should all have in common, though, is the desire to walk closely with God every step of the way. No matter what you're wishing to achieve or accomplish, don't forget to look up at God and recognize that no matter what, He's there. You don't have to reach any goal to make Him proud. He just wants your love. He wants you to know that He's there with you and for you. God wants you to have the same joy when you look at Him that He has when He looks at you. That's the heart of our Heavenly Father. God loves the park, and He loves you even more.

At the end of my life, I want to be able to walk back to the car with some ice cream stains on my shirt, a sunburn on my face, and maybe even some scrapes on my knees, and I want to be able to look up at God from the passenger seat and say, "That was so much fun. I can't wait for you to bring someone else here with you so they can experience the whole thing. Let's go home."

About the Author

Joseph Suggs writes books, which, considering that you're reading this right now, seems to make perfect sense. Dedicated to reaching people who need a reminder that they are loved, he believes the simplicity of the Gospel is something that should be shared with every generation.